# STEWARDSHIP

## GOD'S WAY OF RECREATING THE WORLD

BY

STEVE KINDLE

Energion Publications
Gonzalez, FL
2015

ISBN10: 1-63199-173-6
ISBN13: 978-1-63199-173-8


Energion Publications
P. O. Box 841
Gonzalez, FL 32560

energion.com
pubs@energion.com

To First Christian Church (Disciples of Christ)
of Redding, California
Partners with God in recreating the world


With thanks and appreciation to Larry Haight, Director of
Library Services, and Eric Wheeler, Reader and Digital Services
Librarian for Simpson University, and Keegan Osinski, Public
Services Assistant, Vanderbilt Divinity Library, for their assis-
tance in providing many of the resources for this book.

# INTRODUCTION

There is little disagreement that our world is as close to self-destruction as it has ever been, humanity included. It is unnecessary to list the wars, political conflicts, diseases, ecological disasters, and the like; we are all too familiar with a daily rehearsal of our plight. What there is little or no agreement on is the way out. How will we, as the human race, (homo sapiens, or "the wise humans") find our way out of our mutually shared predicament and into a world of wholeness and abundance that the Hebrews named shalom? Is there any wisdom available to us that can lead the way?

Jews and Christians have at their disposal a wisdom that is comprehensive enough to meet the challenges of our time. We understand this wisdom to be a gift from God as we have received it through the Hebrew and Christian scriptures. The only problem is that we have abandoned it long ago. At least we in the West have, who traded in our bountiful inheritance for a mess of meager pottage known as the consumerist society,[1] and the promotion of the individual over the greater good for all.

This book is a challenge and an appeal. Its challenge is to reconnect with the ancient wisdom that first conceived of a world after God's own heart. Its appeal is to take up the mission we pray so often, "Your will be done on earth as it is in heaven." God's will for God's creation is not hidden or kept solely for the initiate. It is not beyond the ability of the lowliest disciple or too inconsequential for the highest. To rediscover and then implement our sapiential heritage is not only vital, it is our highest calling as humans, and the way out of our current and continuing crisis.

Joseph Blenkinsopp, in his *Creation, Un-creation, Re-creation: A discursive commentary on Genesis 1-11*, outlines the progression of God's activity from the perspective of primordial time to the call

---

1 "Consumerism describes a society in which many people formulate their goals in life partly through acquiring goods that they clearly do not need for subsistence or for traditional display. They become enmeshed in the process of acquisition — shopping — and take some of their identity from a [possession] of new items that they buy and exhibit." Peter N. Stearns, *Consumerism in World History* (London: Routledge, 2006), p. ix.

of Abraham.[2] With the desire of Adam and Eve "to be like God," humanity was set on a course of self-destruction that ended with God being so sorry ("for it repenteth me that I had made them." KJV) that God wiped out all but the necessary ingredients with which to start over, or re-create. From that first moment Noah emerged from the ark, God has been working to return creation, and certainly humanity, to God's original purpose.

Primordial time has become our time: humanity is un-creating our world even as God is hard at work re-creating it. Until humans restore God's original intention for partnership in maintaining the Earth, we will continue on our road to destruction.

The farther we get away from Modernism's tendency to break down everything into its constituent parts, keeping them separate, and move toward seeing the entire universe as one integrated whole, the closer we get to understanding stewardship. The New Physics teaches us that everything is connected and has a relationship to everything else, however remote. Science is hard at work to find the organizing principle to explain how the universe works. Stewardship functions in that regard for Christianity. It is the organizing principle that shows how every other aspect of our faith fits together.

Separating out religion as a discrete part of life is a modern construct and is not the way the early church saw its place in the scheme of things. To ask if a person was religious, even up to the 16th century, was nonsensical. All of life was seen as invested with value and to be taken as a gift of God and used accordingly. Modern life is seen as a series of compartments that we enter one at a time: work, play, spirituality, exercise, family, and so on. So too in congregational life. Sundays (and perhaps Wednesday evenings) are for worship, Monday through Friday are for work, weekends are for family and hobbies. The problem is that when one enters one sphere, one leaves another behind. This complicates churches' efforts to make stewardship a way of life that encompasses every aspect of our lives.

Today our churches struggle with meeting budgets, membership decline, ministry obligations, spiritual transformation,

2   Joseph Blenkinsopp, *Creation, Un-creation, Re-creation: A discursive commentary on Genesis 1-11*(London: Bloomsbury T&T Clark, 2011).

effective evangelism, competing commitments, rapid change, youth exodus, diminishing effectiveness, and the seeming irrelevance of its message. Individual Christians long for deeper connections to God and each other, significant ministry, solutions for our ecological and humanitarian crises, and relevant support through life's vicissitudes.

It is my contention, and the thesis of this book, that stewardship, comprehensively understood and applied, will lead a congregation and individual Christians out of these problems and into mature and effective relationships and significant ministry. And, most importantly of all, it will restore the Earth, and its people, to peace and prosperity.

This is not a "quick fix" book on stewardship; it is much more than that. It is more of a permanent fix when properly understood.

Every pilot flies according to *The Pilot's Handbook of Aeronautical Knowledge*, that is, every pilot who wants to fly safely and most enjoyably. SCUBA divers dive with the knowledge they gained from NAUI or PADI certification instruction; not to do so puts their lives in peril. No explorer ventures forth without first gaining as much knowledge of the territory presently available; not doing so increases the risk of not returning. It behooves us as Christians who desire to walk closely with God to discover just where it is God is walking, or we may find ourselves pursuing irrelevant goals. Karl Barth famously advised young theologians "to take your Bible and take your newspaper, and read both. But interpret newspapers from your Bible."[3] That's another way of saying that how we look at the world should be as close to how God sees it as possible. For Christians (and Jews) this means paying close attention to our Bible.

This is not as easy as it seems on first blush. In a previous book.[4] I discussed how difficult it is to agree on biblical teaching. I suggested a method of interpreting the Bible called a canon within the Canon. This is an effort to approximate or summarize the essence of biblical teaching and compare portions of the Bible to it. Fortunately, for this study, promoting a specific interpretive model is not necessary. I suspect most parties to this discussion will agree

---

3  Time Magazine, Friday, May 31, 1963.
4  *I'm Right and You're Wrong!: Why we disagree about the Bible and what to do about it*, (Gonzales, Florida: Energion Publications, 2015).

with the larger points made, as most models arrive at the same conclusions. So why this book? Because, although most will agree with its understanding of stewardship, few actually incorporate these findings in the day-to-day operation of congregations or in their own lives. Stewardship is seen as a mere tool, not a way of life. This book is a challenge to make stewardship the controlling idea of congregational and individual life.

Those involved with other religions and their adherents soon discover that they all are concerned with the same thing: discovering and promoting the purpose of life. The differences are many and profound in how they go about this, but in the final analysis, they are pursuing their understanding of how to live properly in our world.

This is no less true of Christianity. If you are a Christian, you have a basic understanding of why you are here and what you should be doing with your life. Depending on your denomination or theological understanding, such issues as evangelism, sanctification, liberation, justice seeking, and the like compete for a Christian's first allegiance. Just as with differing biblical interpretations, each one has its able defenders. What we need is a way to make them all essential without having them compete with one another. By broadly applying biblical stewardship principles, each is elevated and transformed.

One of the problems with stewardship as it is taught in our churches today is that it is a "program," and one that is relegated to underwriting the annual budget. So biblical stewardship is undermined in two ways. One, it is seen as being about money, and two, it is just another part of the life of the church. Neither of these is healthy nor helpful. Until stewardship is regarded as a vital aspect of everything that touches the life of the church and individual Christians, we will limp along with mediocre impact on our world and ourselves. Ironically, when stewardship is seen comprehensively, that is, as a way of life, money will no longer be an issue.

One of the "givens" of Christian teaching is that the world is in need of redemption. Judaism teaches us that the world is in need of sanctification, that is, it needs to be regarded as set apart for God's purposes, and appropriately considered. Whether you take a literal view of "The Fall," or regard the Theory of Evolution as more to the point, most agree that the state of our world is dire. Humanity is consumed with hate for the "other," and the planet is on its way to polluting itself to death. Our God, through Christ, is in the redemption business. The "good news of the gospel" is that all forms of oppression, of either individuals or the planet, are in the process of being overcome. When we pray, "Your kingdom come, your will be done on earth as it is in heaven," we are acknowledging our need for radical change in our world and our commitment to assist in this change. However, our work only begins with prayer; it ends with action.

A story is told of a recalcitrant man who continually resisted the urging of the local pastor to attend Sunday worship. The man was a very successful gardener, and his garden was the envy of all who passed by. One day the pastor stopped by to admire the garden and found the man working the ground. "My, what a beautiful garden the Lord has given you, brother." "Well," said the man, "You should have seen this ground when God had it all to himself!"

We will investigate the basis of why God calls upon us humans to partner with God in returning the world to its rightful state, shalom (universal wholeness). God will wave no magic wand over Earth. Only stewardship in its fullest expression can make the earth and us whole again.

# Making God's Priorities Our Priorities

## Psalm 50:10-12

*[E]very wild animal of the forest is mine,*
*the cattle on a thousand hills.*
*I know all the birds of the air,*
*and all that moves in the field is mine.*
*If I were hungry, I would not tell you,*
***for the world and all that is in it is mine.***

The Christian view of God and God's relationship to the world begins where the Bible begins, with the Genesis account of creation. It is also the starting place to understand stewardship in its broadest sense.

In a startling reversal of ancient near eastern stories of creation, beginning with Genesis 1, God creates a universe of benign celestial objects (not gods to be worshiped or feared), and human beings in God's own image (not adversaries or slaves of the gods).

> Then God said, "Let us make humankind in our image, according to our likeness; and let them have dominion over the fish of the sea, and over the birds of the air, and over the cattle, and over all the wild animals of the earth, and over every creeping thing that creeps upon the earth." So God created humankind in his image, in the image of God he created them; male and female he created them. God blessed them, and God said to them, "Be fruitful and multiply, and fill the earth and subdue it; and have dominion over the fish of the sea and over the birds of the air and over every living thing that moves upon the earth." — Genesis 1:26-28

The creator pronounces the world and all that is in it "very good." "*Good*" immediately begs the question, "*Good for what?*" The Hebrew word for "good" טוב *towb*, carries the meaning "appropriate for its purpose." So the creation is deemed very good for the purpose for which God made it. That purpose, in part, is to provide a vocation for humanity, and abundance for all living things who depend upon the earth.

Beginning with Genesis 2:4b, we are introduced to the purpose of humanity through the formation of אָדָם 'adam, "the man." We are told that God places 'adam in a garden (a well-watered place) east, in Eden. It is here that God commissions 'adam: "*The Lord God took the man and put him in the garden of Eden to till it and keep it.*" This commission defines not only the purpose of humans in God's creation scheme, but also the meaning of stewardship: "to till it and to keep it." The Hebrew word for "till" is עָבַד 'abad, normally meaning "to serve." "To keep" is in Hebrew שָׁמַר shamar whose root is "to exercise great care over."[5]

The picture here is one of the Creator creating a world that is intended to provide sustenance for humanity and all other created things, but under the care of God's stewards, human beings. From the beginning, its perpetual preservation was not a given. It depended on how well humans would till it and keep it. Understanding this as a two-part process is essential. They are inseparable for proper understanding of the humans' role as stewards.

"To till it," is to bring out that which it was intended to produce. "To keep it," is to insure that the next steward (generation) will be able to continue tilling (deriving) that for which it is intended. In this way, the succession of generations will have an unbroken bounty to call upon to sustain themselves and all that proper tilling and keeping depends upon. This is the formula for perpetual sustainability.

This has serious implications for understanding how *filling the earth, subduing it, and having dominion over it* are to be interpreted. Whatever else these terms describe, none can be taken to lessen in any way the need to insure that whatever is done will not impact the next generation's ability to derive its proper use.

However, the history of interpretation has not always yielded such a satisfactory result. Having dominion and subduing have led some to believe that the bounty of the earth is for the taking, not considering the effect this has on the planet or its inhabitants (animal, vegetable, and mineral).

In 1962, Rachael Carson wrote a book about the damage DDT and other chemicals were having on birds and other life.

5  Victor P. Hamilton, *The Book of Genesis* (Grand Rapids, Michigan: William B. Eerdmans Publishing Company, 1990), p. 171.

The *Silent Spring* turned the world's attention to ecology in crisis and the environmental movement began. Her focus was mainly on the chemical industry. It remained for Lynn White, Jr., in 1974, to name another culprit, religion, specifically Christianity, in his essay, "The Historical Roots of Our Ecological Crisis."[6]

Here's the summary of White's argument from Douglas Miller.

> Our plight, he argues, stems from the belief in a transcendent God who creates but stands apart from Creation—in contrast with the ancient nature religions that revered the sun, the moon, and Earth's assets. Yahwehism broke the power of sacral mystery within Creation, leaving Nature with no intrinsic value, only instrumental worth. For White, this theology extinguishes eco-affection and holds the Planet hostage to the aggrandizing forces of capitalism that are content to let the market govern its pillage.[7]

To be fair, White named other abettors: emerging nation states,[8] the technological advances prompted by new scientific discoveries, and human hubris. He notes that "human ecology is deeply conditioned by beliefs about nature and destiny—that is, by religion." So, he asks, "What did Christianity tell people about their relations with the environment?" Here's how he sums up the theology that is responsible for our crisis. "Man named all the animals, thus establishing his dominance over them. God planned all this explicitly for man's benefit and rule: no item in the physical creation had any purpose save to serve man's purposes."

Ironically, White suggested that the answer to this anti-planet theology may just come from St. Francis of Assisi. Ironic, because Francis is as well a product of Christian theology. Therefore, White's analysis is but one of several possible outcomes of reading the Genesis story.

---

6  Lynn White, Jr., *Ecology and Religion in History* (New York: Harper and Row, 1974). All White quotes are from this article.

7  Douglas J. Miller, *Jesus Goes to Washington* (Eugene, Oregon: Wipf and Stock Publishers, 2013), p. 28.

8  These newly formed nation-states, in order to survive the competition with one another, literally scoured the world in search of riches to undergird their power and prestige. This began exploitation on a global scale.

White leaves us with a stern warning. "Hence, we shall continue to have a worsening ecological crisis until we reject the Christian axiom that nature has no reason for existence save to serve man." Whether or not he is right in his analysis of cause, he certainly is in respect to the cure. However, I would claim that the problem of treating nature at one's own pleasure is not confined to Christianity, but is prevalent across the world.

White's assessment of Christian culpability is too broad. It may not even be representative, but it surely survives in certain theological quarters. It hasn't been that long since the bounty of the earth seemed inexhaustible, and the idea of overconsumption never occurred to our forbearers. So the notions of "dominion" and "subduing" seemed inevitably linked to the way life was lived. It also didn't seem to do much harm.

But we live in a different world today. Our world is marked by dwindling resources and fierce competition over the spoils. The need to understand the meaning of the Genesis story has never been more important than for our day.

We began this section with Psalm 50. In this psalm the psalmist creates a scene where God calls the worshipers to reflect on who God is (the summoner of all the earth) and who Israel is (a people of the covenant). God's people are called to judgment; they have violated their covenant. So far are they from honoring God, God will not honor their rituals of worship. Their sacrifices and rituals are rejected until they are accompanied by right actions and a spirit of thankfulness for what God provides.

Righteous Jews understood this well and incorporated it into their daily blessing of food. These words were undoubtedly said by Jesus as he "gave thanks" on the night he was betrayed. "Blessed are You, Holy One our God, King of the Universe, who brings forth bread from the earth."[9] In this prayer is the twofold recognition that God is the owner of everything and the provider for everyone.

Why has God the right to demand this recognition? Because God, by virtue of being creator of the world, owns everything in it. No bull or goat or anything that might be sacrificed to God was not already God's. God cannot be given anything that comes

9   Rabbi David Zaslow, *Jesus: First Century Rabbi* (Brewster, Massachusetts: Paraclete Press, 2014), p.xiv.

from the earth; it is already God's. The only thing that remains beyond the grasp of God is Israel's thankfulness as expressed in keeping the covenant. It is only in honoring God's covenant—through thankful obedience—that true worship is offered. This is no less true for those who would worship God today. **What God receives from creation through this thankful obedience is stewardship of the Earth.**

Where do such audacious claims come from? How could this psalmist so easily put these words into the very mouth of God? Because the author of Psalm 50 is steeped in Israel's traditions of creation. The psalmist is expositing on Genesis 1:1, *In the beginning when God created the heavens and the earth*. God is the owner by virtue of being the creator. Humans have failed God because they forgot this (*you who forgot God*), and their relationship to God as owner and they as stewards.

How does Genesis depict the relationship of God to humanity and humanity to God? First of all, by distinguishing between the nature of Adam (humanity) and creatures. Adam is created in the image of God. Given the many options for how to understand what this means, Gerhard von Rad sums up its practical import.

> "...one will admit that the text speaks less of the nature of God's image than of its purpose. There is less said about the gift itself than about the task....Just as powerful earthly kings, to indicate their claim to dominion, erect an image of themselves in the provinces of their empire where they do not personally appear, so man is placed upon earth in God's image as God's sovereign emblem. He is really only God's representative, summoned to maintain and enforce God's claim to dominion over the earth."[10]

Here, then, is what our appointment as stewards means: to treat creation as God would have it. Why humans are elected to this position may be impossible to say. What is possible to say is that we are not given *carte blanche* to treat the creation as if **we** were the creator and its purpose is to serve **our** ends. Quite to the contrary. We are the managers of God's estate and are required to

---

10 Gerhard von Rad, *Genesis: A commentary* (Philadelphia: The Westminster Press, 1972), pp. 59-60.

fulfill our mission as God would have it done through appropriate tilling and keeping.

David Cotter expresses this point well. "To be in God's image means to be blessed with the responsibility of ruling the world in such a way that it is the ordered, good, life-giving place that God intends it to be. As God is to the universe—so humanity is to the world."[11] This is what we are to do as God's stewards.

A word about "subduing" the earth is in order here. The Hebrew word כָּבַשׁ *kabash* does carry the meaning of force and coercion. Rather than give humanity permission to use its representative powers to force its will on the earth, it rather describes the formidable nature of the task. Just as God had to overcome the primordial chaos to create the "very good" world, humans will need to exercise its dominion against the forces of chaos that would take the world back to "without form and void" if we let it. Stewardship is not easy, and it is not without severe opposition, yet we have all the tools necessary for the task if we rely on God's intentions and not our own.

---

11 David W. Cotter, *Genesis* (Collegeville, Minnesota: The Liturgical Press, 2003) p.18.

# THE WORLD AS GOD WOULD HAVE IT: THE SCOPE OF STEWARDSHIP

As we progress through Genesis and note how the creation stories shaped Israel's understanding of humanity's place in God's world, all is well until we reach the third chapter. There we discover a description of the three conditions that have dogged humanity throughout time. Humans are now alienated from God, the land, and one another.

The one prohibition in the Garden was not to eat of the tree of knowledge of good and evil. (2:17) When God inquired of Adam, "Where are you?" (3:9) we see the beginning of the chasm that spiritually separates humanity from God. Adam actually blames God for his transgression by claiming that "the woman whom you gave to be with me," (3:12) is responsible. By throwing Eve under the bus, humans are now estranged from each other. In the "curse" of the ground (3:17), which no longer provides abundantly for humanity, humans must now labor intensely for their food, and the creatures suffer along with them. This is a picture of humanity having to fend for itself. Terrible consequences ensue that are so heinous to God that God resolves to destroy every living thing and start over again. This is a world that turned against God and removed itself thoroughly from God's intentions.

Yet, God has declared these alienations reconciled; the hostilities are over.

> *All this is from God, who reconciled us to himself through Christ, and has given us the ministry of reconciliation; that is, in Christ God was reconciling the world to himself, not counting their trespasses against them, and entrusting the message of reconciliation to us.* — 2 Corinthians 5:18-19

Stewards are the ambassadors of God who bring this message of peace to the world as they model God's reconciliation.

I remember, as a young man, watching an old movie called, *All Quiet on the Western Front,* made from a book by a Erich Maria Remarque. It's about three friends, German soldiers, who happened to be stationed together in France during WWI. In the heat of a battle, the main character, Paul Bäumer, ducked into a crater made from a mortar shell and found himself face to face with a French soldier. He instinctively pulled out his knife and killed him.

In the boredom and relief of a safe place, Bäumer began to wonder about this enemy of his. He rummaged through his uniform and pulled out his wallet. After a few minutes, he spoke to the deceased French soldier.

> "Comrade, I did not want to kill you. . . . But you were only an idea to me before, an abstraction that lived in my mind and called forth its appropriate response. . . . I thought of your hand-grenades, of your bayonet, of your rifle; now I see your wife and your face and our fellowship. Forgive me, comrade. We always see it too late. Why do they never tell us that you are poor devils like us, that your mothers are just as anxious as ours, and that we have the same fear of death, and the same dying and the same agony—Forgive me, comrade; how could you be my enemy?"

Bäumer utters these words to the corpse of Gérard Duval. He realizes for the first time that, despite the propaganda of war, Duval is fundamentally no different from him. As Duval becomes a fully realized person in Bäumer's mind, he thinks beyond the man's weapons to "your wife and your face and our fellowship." Once he understands Duval as a human being, the artificial divisions between the two men become irrelevant and they are now one in their common humanity. This is what God wants us all to know about each other. Human tragedy begins when we believe our differences are more important than what we have in common.

At the end of the story, Paul is walking away from the war as it had just been declared over. But an enemy plane came out of the sky and killed him. Yes, the war, the hostility between humans created in the image of God, is declared over by God in Jesus Christ, but the hostility continues.

Douglas Hall assess the depths of change necessary to avoid an ecological and human Armageddon.

> There can be no serious or permanent alteration of the catastrophic course upon which civilization is set without a metanoia [repentance, or turning around and going the other way] in the soul of First World peoples....For the changes that

13

are requisite for planetary survival and shalom are not surface rearrangements like the redistribution of material goods and service, but a transformation at the level of personal and social being. In short, we must get a new image of ourselves: we ourselves must be changed![12]

He is joined in this by one of America's leading Christian ethicists, Douglas Miller. He writes, "Our global predicament is fed by a massive moral failure. Thus, every effort in achieving a just society and a renewable biosphere will languish without changing our fundamental values."[13]

Mohandas Gandhi, one of the most influential figures in modern social and political activism, considered these traits to be the most spiritually perilous to humanity:

- Wealth without Work
- Pleasure without Conscience
- Science without Humanity
- Knowledge without Character
- Politics without Principle
- Commerce without Morality
- Worship without Sacrifice

Each of these describes a feature of the pervasive moral failure at work in our world. Each is also the opposite of good stewardship, and collectively, their source is a product of the three alienations now operating in our world. Briefly, here's how:

**Wealth without Work**: Taking from your neighbor that which is rightfully your neighbor's.

**Pleasure without Conscience**: Disregarding the needs of others as we satisfy our own.

**Science without Humanity**: Unleashing on an unsuspecting pubic terrors beyond imagining.

**Knowledge without Character**: Selling our souls to the highest bidder regardless of its use.

---

12 Douglas John Hall, *Imaging God: Dominion as Stewardship*, (Grand Rapids: Wm. B. Eerdmans Publishing Co., 1986), p. 13.
13 Douglas J. Miller, *Op cit,* p.1.

14

**Politics without Principle**: Doing what it takes to get reelected, not respecting the people.

**Commerce without Morality**: Producing shoddy and unhealthy products because they sell.

**Worship without Sacrifice**: Choosing one's religion for what it can do for you.

The plaintive cry of the old Latin hymn resonates today.

> O come, O come, Emanuel, and ransom captive Israel,
> That mourns in lonely exile here,
> Until the Son of God appear.

The import of this hymn is that there is nothing humanity can do to return us from exile, that is, the terrible conditions of oppression, injustice, and ecological waste that threaten existence until Jesus returns. This is only partly true. We are in exile, meaning, living away from the intentions of God for creation, but we do have a model for returning to abundance and justice for all.

# The World as God Would Have It: Jubilee

So, what would the world look like if God's intentions were universally applied? To answer this question, we need to look at God's model for the world, Israel, as elaborated in the Torah and reflected upon by the Prophets, and re-inaugurated by Jesus in the kingdom of God.

Jesus did not appear out of a vacuum; his life was carefully shaped by his deeply religious family, his devotion to the Torah, and careful listening to the words of the Prophets. His debt to these is seen in the recitation of his core values in Luke 4.

> *18 The Spirit of the Lord is upon me, because he has anointed me to bring good news to the poor. He has sent me to proclaim release to the captives and recovery of sight to the blind, to let the oppressed go free, 19 to proclaim the year of the Lord's favor.*

When Jesus announced his ministry as the onset of "the year of the Lord's favor," he was recalling the centerpiece of the Torah's vision of the world as God would have it, as found in Deuteronomy 25-26. It's well-named the Year of Jubilee, as it certainly was a time of jubilation for Israel.

In the Jubilee, there is *release* for those reduced to poverty because of debts ("good news to the poor"), a *redistribution* of lands lost to usury and injustice that made the poor chattel to the rich ("proclaim release to the captives"), Sabbath *rest* for land and people ("let the oppressed go free"), and in general, a new beginning for everyone. The kingdom of God in Jesus' hands is the proclamation of Jubilee for all the earth.

This was not lost on the early Christians. The Book of Acts records the practice of the Jesus people as *All who believed were together and had all things in common; they would sell their possessions and goods and distribute the proceeds to all, as any had need* (Acts 2:44-45).

The Jubilee year was the fiftieth year since the last Jubilee. In between Jubilees, other practices were put in place that mitigated the effects of greed and oppression. Peter Vogt lists three humanitarian principles that undergird the Torah's concern for justice not only for humans but for creatures as well. These are laws emphasize the value of human life and human dignity, laws dealing with interpersonal social relations, and laws dealing with the humane treatment of animals.[14]

The principal protections of the poor can be easily summarized.[15]

- *Gleanings and Harvests:* The corners of fields and the grapes dropped by the workers were reserved for the poor (Deuteronomy 24:17; Leviticus 19:9-10). The poor were also allowed to eat from land that lay fallow or idle in the Sabbath years (Leviticus 25:1-7; Deuteronomy 15:1-11).
- *Protection from Creditors:* Creditors could not charge interest or keep garments (which provided warmth and doubled as one's blanket at night), nor could they take the tools of a man's trade as security for a loan. These provisions ensured people's ability to earn a living and also prevented extreme hardships (Exodus 22:25-27; Deuteronomy 24:12-13).
- *Right to Timely Wages:* The poor worker, whether a stranger or brother, was to receive his wages on the day of his labor, all the more so if he had need of it immediately (Leviticus 19:13; Deuteronomy 24:14-15).
- *Year of Jubilee:* Once every 50 years, Jubilee provided a comprehensive program of debt cancellation, liberation from indentured servitude, and the complete restoration of each family's ancestral property, granting the poor a fresh start (Leviticus 25:8-22).
- *Kinsman Redeemer:* Family members were to help each other repurchase their land if they fell into debt and lost it (Leviticus 25:23-34). Family members could also purchase freedom for one another if they were forced into slavery to meet financial needs (Leviticus 25:47-55). Widows could also be saved from their plight by kinsman redeemers, as in the case of Boaz's aid to Ruth and her mother-in-law Naomi (Ruth 4:1-10).

---

14 Peter T. Vogt, "Social Justice and the Vision of Deuteronomy," *JETS* 51/1 (March 2008) pp. 35–44.

15 This list is from Ryan Casselberry, "Giving in the Old Testament: The Poor and Needy." Generous Giving Ministry, http://library.generousgiving.org/page.asp?sec=28&page=. This site is no longer available.

- *The Right to Rest:* Servants, slaves, strangers and even animals were to participate in the Sabbath (Deuteronomy 5:1-15).
- *Scaled Prices for Sacrifices and Offerings:* Poor people who could not afford to present costly sacrifices and offerings were allowed to sacrifice less costly sacrifices that they could afford (Leviticus 5:7, 11; 14:21).
- *The Tithe:* One of the tithes was collected with a particular command to include aliens, the fatherless, widows and other poor people in a yearly community feast and celebration (Deuteronomy 14:22-29).

These obligations of Israel toward their neighbors (including aliens) were deeply ingrained in Jesus, as reflected in his attitude and behavior toward all. The rabbis teach that the Torah is both the mediator of God and the focus of God's presence. Jesus, as the ultimate revealer of God for Christians, imbued the Torah and become the personification of God.

Vogt concludes,

> Rather than being an example of secularization, in which care for the marginal groups and the poor is mandated almost entirely on humanitarian and compassionate grounds, Deuteronomy's call to social justice is based on the fact that the people of Israel are the people of Yahweh. As such, they are called to live out that relationship in radically counter-cultural ways. They are to serve as a paradigm for the rest of humanity, demonstrating to a watching world what it means to be the people of God.

If the world is watching Christians, what are they seeing? Are we following in the tradition of Israel that was so beautifully captured in the life and mission of Jesus?

Walter Brueggemann, building on the magisterial works of Abraham Heschel[16] and Michael Fishbane,[17] finds in the keeping

---

16 Abraham Heschel, *The Sabbath: It's Meaning for Modern Man* (New York: Farrar, Straus, Giroux, 1951).

17 Michael Fishbane, *Sacred Attunement: A Jewish Theology* (Chicago: University of Chicago Press, 2008).

of the Sabbath a model for how Christians should comport them-selves in the world.[18]

It is not asking too much of the Sabbath to be the most im-portant instructor in doing the work of the steward, for the final act of the creation story is the creation of the Sabbath. It serves there to model the *telos* or purpose of creation: to give rest to all things. God and creation at rest: the very picture of shalom, the world's optimum state.

However, no commandment seems more outdated and remote to modern sensibilities than keeping the Sabbath day holy. Yet, no commandment serves to ennoble our lives more and offer hope for human well-being. Just as the First Commandment helps us order our lives around the most meaningful priorities, so the Fourth Commandment provides for our physical, mental, and spiritual well-being as individuals in community and offers a vision of com-plete well-being for the cosmos.

---

18 Walter Brueggemann, *Sabbath as Resistance: Saying no to the culture of now* (Louisville, KY : Westminster John Knox Press, 2014).

# Misconceptions about Stewardship

As long as we make stewardship mainly about money, we will miss the larger emphasis that is necessary for us to bring alienated parties together, transcend our current ecological predicament, and create peace and abundance in our world. Contributing to the overemphasis on money are several interpretations of scripture that tend to make money the central issue.

## The Rich Ruler

Perhaps the best known of these is the "Rich Ruler" in Luke 18:18-26. *A certain ruler asked him* [Jesus], *"Good Teacher, what must I do to inherit eternal life?"* Jesus rehearsed some of the commandments with him, to which the ruler replied, *"I have kept all these since my youth." When Jesus heard this, he said to him, "There is still one thing lacking. Sell all that you own and distribute the money to the poor, and you will have treasure in heaven; then come, follow me." ²³But when he heard this, he became sad; for he was very rich.*

This story is too often used to decry wealth per se, when its intention is to call this ruler into judgment for not considering the poor as part of his obligation of being wealthy. The middle class in the West are prone not to think of themselves as wealthy, yet their standard of living is the envy of most of the world. So the average Christian reading this biblical encounter think it's about someone else. This is a cautionary tale to all of us who lavish our wealth only on ourselves and reserve for the poor only crumbs from our tables.

## Zacchaeus

Lest we get carried away by the wholesale renunciation of wealth and make it apply to all rich (or even the well-off), we need to set the encounter with the rich ruler alongside another encounter with a rich man in Luke 19, Zacchaeus. Here's the story:

> He entered Jericho and was passing through it. ²A man was there named Zacchaeus; he was a chief tax collector and was rich. ³He was trying to see who Jesus was, but on account of the crowd he could not, because he was short in stature. ⁴So he ran

*ahead and climbed a sycamore tree to see him, because he was going to pass that way.⁵When Jesus came to the place, he looked up and said to him, "Zacchaeus, hurry and come down; for I must stay at your house today."⁶So he hurried down and was happy to welcome him. ⁷All who saw it began to grumble and said, "He has gone to be the guest of one who is a sinner."⁸Zacchaeus stood there and said to the Lord, "Look, half of my possessions, Lord, I will give to the poor; and if I have defrauded anyone of anything, I will pay back four times as much."⁹Then Jesus said to him, "Today salvation has come to this house, because he too is a son of Abraham."*

In contrast to the rich ruler, Jesus asked nothing from him, yet Zacchaeus offered "half" his wealth to the poor, and restitution to those he defrauded.

In neither case do we have a template to impose upon all rich or well-off people. Jesus, it seems, took everyone on a case-by-case basis. In the rich ruler, he determined that, regardless of his devotion to the commandments, he missed the bigger picture of solidarity with the oppressed. In order for the ruler to inherit eternal life, that is, to enter the kingdom of God, his priorities needed to be severely altered to comprehend his present distance from it.

On the other hand, Zacchaeus got it. How, we cannot say, as Luke left this out. But he immediately altered his life's orientation and became a good steward.

In our day, we have seen remarkable turnarounds in wealthy people, such as Microsoft founder Bill Gates, who give billions to worthy causes to end disease, hunger, and educate children. The issue then, as now, is not wealth, but what we do with it.

## THE WIDOW'S MITE

Perhaps as well known is the story of the "Widows Mite" (KJV) or "copper coins" (NRSV).

*[Jesus]sat down opposite the treasury, and watched the crowd putting money into the treasury. Many rich people put in large sums. ⁴²A poor widow came and put in two small copper coins, which are worth a penny. ⁴³Then he called his disciples and said to them, "Truly I tell you, this poor widow has put in more than all those who are contributing to the treasury. ⁴⁴For all of them*

*have contributed out of their abundance; but she out of her poverty has put in everything she had, all she had to live on."* — Mark 12:41-44

It is easy to move from this story to say that the ideal is to take a vow of poverty and give all we have to God. After all, didn't Jesus highly commend the widow for her sacrificial giving?

Maybe not. Two things work against this interpretation. One is the immediate context where Jesus excoriates the scribes, in part, for they "devour widow's houses." Jesus wants widows to keep their homes, not reduce themselves to poverty. His observation in v. 44 may be a continuation of his rebuke of the scribes for reducing this woman into poverty, noting that the scribes contribute out of the widow's misfortune.

We also need to recall that Jesus insisted that we not tempt the Lord our God. Isn't this what we do when we voluntarily reduce ourselves to poverty and then expect God to make our lives manageable? Even for those in the Roman Catholic Church, and others, who take a vow of poverty, they are really committing themselves to a subsistence living that is underwritten by the selfless service of a supportive community. They are not destitute.

## JESUS VERSUS CAESAR:
### THE CONFLICT OF TWO KINGDOMS IN LUKE 20

This confrontation of Jesus on the temple grounds with chief priests, scribes, and elders, has been interpreted over the centuries to endorse the notion that there are two spheres in which humans operate, the kingdom of God and the kingdom of Caesar. We owe allegiance to each kingdom in proportion to what is theirs. This has come down to our day as the religious and secular spheres of life.

*[20]So they watched him and sent spies who pretended to be honest, in order to trap him by what he said, so as to hand him over to the jurisdiction and authority of the governor. [21]So they asked him, "Teacher, we know that you are right in what you say and teach, and you show deference to no one, but teach the way of God in accordance with truth. [22]Is it lawful for us to pay taxes to the emperor, or not?"[23]But he perceived their craftiness and said to them, [24]"Show me a denarius. Whose head and whose title does it*

*bear?" They said, "The emperor's." *<sup>25</sup>*He said to them, "Then give
to the emperor the things that are the emperor's, and to God the
things that are God's." *<sup>26</sup>*And they were not able in the presence of
the people to trap him by what he said; and being amazed by his
answer, they became silent.*

So what are we to make of Jesus' pronouncement, *Then give
to the emperor the things that are the emperor's, and to God the things
that are God's?*

The starting place is to note the circumstance that brought the
question of paying taxes to Jesus. This was not a question posed
to gain a legitimate answer from a man the questioners honored.
Rather, it was posed by spies to trap Jesus. How so?

The trap was this: Had Jesus answered, "Yes, it is right to pay
taxes to Caesar," he would have lost his authority with his Jewish
followers who hated the Romans and loathed the temple tax. On
the other hand, had he said, "No, paying taxes to Caesar is forbid-
den," he would have been immediately arrested by the temple guard
and likely led to an untimely crucifixion. Either answer would have
sprung the trap his enemies laid for him.

Jesus was more than a match to his adversaries. The answer
he gave satisfied both the Romans and Jews. As for the Romans,
they interpreted Jesus to mean, "Yes, by all means, pay to Caesar
what is his." As for the Jews, they heard Jesus to mean, "Yes, by
all means, pay to Caesar what is his, which, of course, is nothing,
since everything is God's." It's no wonder the spies were awed into
silence and bothered him no more.

But, one may object, using Paul's admonition in Romans 13,
that governments derive their authority from God, and that Christians are subject to their authority.

Note this significant statement. "For rulers are not a terror to
good conduct, but to bad." Paul would have a very difficult time
convincing the author of the Revelation of John of this, or Dietrich
Bonhoeffer of Nazi Germany, or any number of victims of repres-
sive regimes imprisoned or killed for doing the right thing. So some
would limit Paul's admonition to "good governments" that actually
do God's work. But, I would ask, is there such a government? To

have to determine the good from the bad is an impossible task and, therefore, makes following Paul here impossible as well.

I classify Romans 13 along with Paul's accommodation of slavery, occasional subordination of women, and his advice not to marry if at all possible, to his belief in the immanent return of Jesus in his or his generation's lifetime. Given that the world will soon be governed by Jesus in all righteousness, justice, and peace, there is no need to oppose slavery, the inequality of women, earthly governments, or to form a family. Relief is just around the corner.

We are diverted from stewardship when we believe a political solution can solve our problems. The "Great Society" envisioned by president Lyndon Johnson is only a pale shadow of God's intention for the world. Governments, which operate largely out of their own "self-interests," are incapable of ushering in shalom. Governments, which are actually biblical "principalities and powers," are objects of stewardship, not solutions.[19]

## TITHING

I have no particular reason for objecting to tithing beyond it being an arbitrary way to determine an amount appropriate for God. (No one really knows the percentage of giving required under Mosaic Law.)[20] At least tithers (those who give 10% of their income) are giving, and giving well above the average giver. And tithing is often seen as the top of the giving ladder when so many are capable of so much more. But the question posed to which tithing can be an answer is the wrong question. "How much should I give," should be recalculated to "How much should I keep for myself?" Stewards who know *whose* it is that they are charged with managing, will want to do the most they can with all they have. The criterion for "How much" is "How well am I tilling and keeping?" A good rule of thumb is John Wesley's dictum, "Earn all you can,

---

19 See the *Powers* trilogy of Walter Wink for a thorough analysis of why this is true.

20 For a comprehensive look at all the arguments, pro and con, for tithing, see David A. Croteau's *Tithing after the Cross* (Gonzales, Florida: Energion Publications, 2013).

save all you can, give all you can." All of which must be understood through good stewardship practices.

The questions around how much to give are too often reserved for "Stewardship Drives." So we compartmentalize our giving and tuck it away for another year. In all the talk of stewardship, seldom does it go much beyond the pocketbook. Whenever stewardship is reduced to a program, something is terribly wrong, and congregations and individuals continue to struggle.

The apostle Paul revealed to us the key to successful fundraising in his appeal to the Corinthian congregation to assist in the collection he was taking up for the Jerusalem church. His formula: *³For, as I can testify, they voluntarily gave according to their means, and even beyond their means, ⁴begging us earnestly for the privilege of sharing in this ministry to the saints— ⁵and this, not merely as we expected; they gave themselves first to the Lord and, by the will of God, to us,...* — 2 Corinthians 8:3-5

The Macedonians, in spite of their poverty, begged to give to the Jerusalem church—even beyond their means—**because they first gave themselves to the Lord**. Sure, it is possible to raise a lot of money using sophisticated methods based on psychological triggers and emotional appeals. These are too often resorted to as substitutes for the Macedonian way. A congregation that first "gives themselves to the Lord," recognizes their stewardship partnership, and everything they do springs from that commitment. So let's not encourage tithing, that's about money. Let's encourage seeing all we have as God's and act accordingly.

# INHIBITIONS TO
# COMPREHENSIVE STEWARDSHIP

## A FALSE DICHOTOMY BETWEEN LOVING GOD AND LOVING THE WORLD (*KOSMOS*)

The history of Christianity discloses myriad approaches to the Christian's relationship to the world including ascetic denial of all things not spiritual and removal of life to the desert; its opposite: aggressive spiritual warfare against all things worldly; an aloofness typified by indifference; and in our day, an antagonism toward the world bordering on hatred.

It may come down to observing the distinction between the world as "creation" and the world as "flesh." The former to be loved, the latter to be wary of. Paul's admonition in Romans 12:1 in J. B. Phillips' rendering: "Don't let the world around you squeeze you into its own mould, but let God re-mould your minds from within" is particularly apt here. We are to turn toward God who transforms us from "worldy" ways, into the image of Christ.

In assessing the state of the problem, H. Richard Niebuhr observed that two thousand years of engagement with the world has not brought clarity to the issue, and that the church remains quite divided on the question.[21] I will not attempt to solve this dilemma here, but point to certain realities that impact on stewardship, especially in praxis.

In order for there to be such a thing as caring for the world, it seems to me that the first order of business is to care (have a positive attitude) for the world. Else, why would anyone want to do anything good for it? Since stewardship is a derivative of God's relationship to creation, God's caring for creation must become our own.

"For God so loved the world..." is apparently not enough for some Christians. They reduce its meaning from loving the creation to only loving the people. Actually, that is a sufficient reason to base stewardship on, as one cannot love people without preserving the very source of life itself, by proper tilling and keeping.

---

21 H. Richard Niebuhr, *Christ and Culture* (New York: Harper & Brothers, 1951) p. 2.

Yet, we have theologies that order the lives of millions of Christians that teach people to abhor the world, that it is the domain of Satan, and that Jesus wants nothing more than to destroy it and all the evil it holds.[22] Holding beliefs like these will inhibit one's desire to be a steward. Even certain televangelists are on record condemning Middle Eastern peace talks because any resolution that brings peace will retard the second coming of Jesus.[23]

If the world is despised by God, about to be destroyed, and in the hands of Satan, why would any devout believer want to aid and abet conserving the Earth? Fortunately, there are many more conservative Christians who are not impressed with this negative view of the world and are pitching in, in a variety of ways and movements, to help restore the Earth to sustainability.[24]

## THE FAILURE OF CONGREGATIONS TO TEACH STEWARDSHIP AS A WAY OF LIFE

A blurb on the back of a book on stewardship states, "Valuable new resource for congregations concerned about stewardship." That's just the problem; for too many congregations, stewardship is an option, at least stewardship in the restricted sense. It's tied too closely to money, restricted to budget time and issues, identified with programs and (sometimes) gimmicks, too often attached to lesser motives. Rhodes Thompson chastises the church by claiming, "Surprisingly, the church is responsible for leading the word stewardship astray. Brainwashed from pulpit and pew, stewardship has traded its vocation of serving the world for a preoccupation with saving the church. Not until it is rescued from this ... can stewardship share in God's 'healing of the nations' (Rev. 22:2)."[25]

The question of first importance to a follower of Jesus is, "Do you believe that Jesus is the Christ, the Son of the living God?" The

---

22 Consider, for instance, the *Left Behind* series. And Hal Lindsey's, *The Late, Great Planet Earth*.

23 E.g., Jack van Impe, John Hagee, and Pat Robertson.

24 E.g., Jim Wallace and the *Sojourners* magazine.

25 Rhodes Thompson, *Stewards Shaped by Grace* (St. Louis: Chalice Press, 1990), p. vii.

second is, "What is your primary purpose in the kingdom?" I hope that the answer is to be a steward of God's creation.

## THE LACK OF TRUE COMMUNITY IN OUR CONGREGATIONS

There is great resistance in the West, and particularly in America, to the notion that "It takes a village." The saying refers to raising a child, but it can be applied to almost any human endeavor. The reality is that no one makes it on one's own. We aren't self-educated (who wrote the books Lincoln studied?), we don't make the products we sell in our stores (or print the newspaper our ads are in), and the protections we need come from the taxes of others. Consequently, we regard "doing it yourself" as superior to having to ask for help. This has serious consequences for churches, to say nothing of society. Congregations tend to be a gathering of individuals, not members one of another.

Modern Americans are inheritors of "the rugged individual" ethic that celebrates the notions of "pulling oneself up by one's bootstraps," and "the self-made man." This has led to the feeling that needing help is a character flaw, and providing help is to go out of one's way. So poor people are considered lazy, the handicapped are disadvantaged, the addicted have no self-control, and the undereducated just didn't try hard enough. After all, it's just a matter of applying oneself in America; hard work will reap the American dream of success. This is the result of placing the value of the individual over the need of community. It's only in a crisis that we understand our need for each other. Well, we are in crisis time!

Living in true community is the goal of the work of stewardship. For true community is where everyone lives for the sake of each other. When life is lived this way, everyone wins, and so does the Earth. If each decision we make is based on how it will affect the others I live with (moving out from my biological family, to my church family, to my human family, to the Earth), and their decisions all take me into consideration along with all the others, life will be lived on its highest level. Until this is the focus of the congregation, "stewardship" will remain a "program" and the great work of restoring the creation will have to wait for another day.

# Scriptural Resources
## for Teaching Stewardship

### The Lord's Supper

> *Whoever, therefore, eats the bread or drinks the cup of the Lord in an unworthy manner will be answerable for the body and blood of the Lord.* [28]*Examine yourselves, and only then eat of the bread and drink of the cup.* [29]*For all who eat and drink without discerning the body, eat and drink judgment against themselves.*
> — 1 Corinthians 11:27-29

For most Christians, the observance of the Lord's Supper (Communion, Eucharist, Lord's Table) is the place where divinity and humanity meet most closely. Paul's admonitions to the Corinthians enhance our understanding of the role of stewardship as seen in the proper and improper way for Christians to conduct themselves, not just at the table, but also beyond.

Two phrases capture our stewardship motif, discerning the body, and in an unworthy manner. The Corinthian congregation was in turmoil, divided over leadership issues and certain teachings. There was mistrust, to say the least, and overt hostility toward many. It's in this context that Paul highlights the unchristian behavior and provides a remedy.

The Lord's Supper in Corinth was apparently celebrated in connection with a communal meal, what we today would call a potluck. People would bring food to be shared in common. However, some ignored the others and, going first, would eat much beyond their fair share. They even partook of so much of the wine that they were inebriated. This led those who were delayed not having enough to eat or drink. Paul chastised them with *What! Do you not have homes to eat and drink in? Or do you show contempt for the church of God and humiliate those who have nothing?* The abundance of food was to make sure that the poorest among them would be cared for, in keeping with Jesus' stewardship ethic of caring for all. The behavior of the gluttons displayed a lack of concern for proper stewardship (not discerning the body); therefore, they were behaving in an unworthy manner. This was unworthy of a steward of the Lord who placed them in charge of proper distribution of our daily bread. A "worthy manner" takes into consideration the body of Christ, and discerns its needs. So, to discern the body (meaning those in the body of Christ) is to take one another into consideration. If the practice of stewardship is anything, it is the care of the community, seeing that all are properly looked after.

The purpose of the church is to teach and model the two Great Commandments: *"You shall love the Lord your God with all your heart, and with all your soul, and with all your mind."* [38] *This is the greatest and first commandment.* [39] *And a second is like it: "You shall love your neighbor as yourself"* (Matt. 22:37-39). By not *discerning the body* by their *"unworthy manor,"* they failed on both counts.

## THE LORD'S (STEWARD'S) PRAYER [26]

> *Our Father in heaven, hallowed be your name. Your kingdom come. Your will be done, on earth as it is in heaven. Give us this day our daily bread. And forgive us our debts, as we also have forgiven our debtors. And do not bring us to the time of trial, but rescue us from the evil one.*

*Our Father in heaven* reminds us that our allegiances are to our Creator, and that we are to follow God's lead in the world. And this is "our" Father, as we live in community.

*hallowed be your name* is accomplished by obedience to God's will.

*Your kingdom come. Your will be done, on earth as it is in heaven* reiterates the steward's mission, to assist God in recreating the world after God's own heart.

*Give us this day our daily bread* reminds us that our livelihood comes from God by way of the Earth, and that this happens by proper tilling and keeping.

*And forgive us our debts, as we also have forgiven our debtors* is to live in Jubilee in all aspects of our lives.

---

26 I understand this prayer originated as a way to overcome the oppression of the Roman Empire, but it must not be restricted to that alone. Its phrases encompass so much more.

*And do not bring us to the time of trial, but rescue us from the evil one* serves to reorient our thinking away from serving ourselves or the oppressive forces of the world.

# A STEWARDSHIP SERMON

## "Enough Is Enough!"
### Deuteronomy 5:12-15; Luke 4:16-21

There were moments in human history after which the world was never the same.

» The Roman Empire falling to the barbarians
» The Copernican altering of Earth's place in the universe from its center to virtual obscurity amidst billions and billions of galaxies
» Hiroshima—when the world realized it could destroy itself
» For America, the date September 11, 2001

You may not realize this, but we are in the midst of a world-altering moment: If the world does not catch up to it, our world will never be the same again. Some say it's already too late. I am, of course, referring to the global ecological crisis. The simple reality is that the Industrial Revolution has been so successful that it's on the verge of destroying life on the planet as we know it.

Very few people doubt the truth of this statement; the doubters are largely those who continue to gain from its excesses and want them to continue: the super-capitalists and their allies. So, I'm not going to rehearse the overwhelming evidence here. I take it as a given.

However, even if you disagree with me, I'd like you to stay tuned to the rest of this sermon, as, even if the world's leading scientists are wrong, life can be much improved for us all in returning to the vision that our God has for us and the planet.

That vision is embedded in the story of Moses and Israel and in the self-described agenda of Jesus Christ.

Why should we care about what Moses had to say? After all, 3000 years have passed and the world has moved on from primitive thinking. Really?

Have we moved on from "Thou shalt not kill?" Or commit adultery? Or steal?

Have we moved on from "love your neighbor?" Or not bearing false witness at trial?

I think we have to agree that enduring truths are such because they are worthwhile, regardless of the century or people that brought them to us.

Some, including many Christians, would put keeping the Sabbath in the obsolete category.

That's only because we have lost touch with its original intention, and that if we were to regain it, it would revolutionize our relationship to the Earth and to each other. Yes, revolutionize!

To better appreciate the Sabbath, let's translate it into its modern counterpart: "Economics 101." For keeping the Sabbath meant not just being idle for a day, but returning to God's vision for the world. A vision rooted deeply in economic well-being.

Theologian Douglas Meeks insists that God's primary role in the Bible is as an Economist.[27] God's actions toward Israel and in Jesus seek to insure a world where all have the resources necessary for life. That is to say, enough—only that which we are capable of properly stewarding, and not any more. As Gandhi liked to put it, "The earth has enough for everybody's need, but not enough for everyone's greed."

It all begins with the story of the creation of Adam and his purpose. Adam was placed by God in the garden "to till it and to keep it." Not to own it; not to exploit it; but to till it (to bring out that which it was intended to produce) and to keep it (that is, to ensure that those who came after him would be able to benefit as well from it). We call this stewardship; not ownership. Adam was commissioned as the first steward of God's marvelous creation. His calling is the calling of every humans since.

The Bible is very clear on who is the owner: the Creator. *For every wild animal of the forest is mine, the cattle on a thousand hills. I know all the birds of the air, and all that moves in the field is mine. If I were hungry, I would not tell you, **for the world and all that is in it is mine*** (Psa. 50).

So what does a world that is owned by God look like?

Throughout the Torah and as witnessed to by the prophets, God is shown to be deeply concerned for economic justice and economic well-being for all people. Here are but a few of the concerns:

---

27 Meeks, M. Douglas. *God the Economist*. Minneapolis, MN: Fortress Press, 1989.

» There is no private property, only stewardship of a fair share
» Everyone is given an equal piece of property to "till and to keep."
» The produce of which is to be shared by all after one has taken enough
» The edges of the crops were not to be harvested, so the poor could scavenge
» Only one pass at harvesting was allowed, for the same reason
» One could not loan money at interest
» One could not refuse a loan to a neighbor
» One could not keep clothing or one's means of production as collateral
» Widows and orphans were given special consideration as they did not have the means to fend for themselves

To keep Israel from forgetting that its role is that of the steward, God gave the Sabbath. For the essence of the Sabbath is this: We rest from our labors to remember that it is God who keeps our lives, and to resist overconsumption (the taking of that which should rightfully go to another).

As you might expect, greed overtook many, and income inequality took hold with great wealth and great poverty living side by side.

Jesus experienced this first-hand as a subject of the Roman Empire.

In Rome, at the time of Jesus, as in America of today, some 2 percent of the population, including the emperor and his family, controlled about 50 percent of the wealth. Another 5 percent, the Senators and land owners, worked in collusion with the emperor. They accounted for up to 30 percent of the wealth. Then, as now, 85 percent to 90 percent of the people were at the bottom of the pile.

It's like this: If there are 100 people in our worship service today and we all ordered pizza delivered for lunch, and 100 slices arrived, six people would take 85 slices and the rest of us (94) would fight over the remaining 15. Yes, fight. That's the price of scarcity.

Jesus died, or rather, was executed by the state, because he taught against this oligarchical system, against the powers and principalities of oppression, and preached an egalitarian Kingdom of God founded on Sabbath Economics.

Hear again our text, from Luke. *The Spirit of the Lord is upon me, because he has anointed me to bring good news to the poor. He has sent me to proclaim release to the captives and recovery of sight to the blind, to let the oppressed go free, to proclaim the year of the Lord's favor.*

This is the message of the Jubilee, the "year of the Lord's favor." This is the message of how God wants the world to work. This is the message Jesus lived and preached that became the message of the kingdom of God.

In the Jubilee, there is *release* for those reduced to poverty because of debts ("good news to the poor"), a *redistribution* of lands lost to usury and injustice that made the poor chattel to the rich ("proclaim release to the captives"), Sabbath *rest* for land and people ("let the oppressed go free"), and in general, a new beginning for everyone. The kingdom of God in Jesus' hands is the proclamation of Jubilee for all the earth.

This was not lost on the early Christians. The Book of Acts records the practice of the Jesus people as *All who believed were together and had all things in common; they would sell their possessions and goods and distribute the proceeds to all, as any had need* (Acts 2:44-45).

Paul got the sense of this in his plea for help from the well-to-do churches to aid the poor, famine struck churches in Jerusalem. *For if the eagerness is there, the gift is acceptable according to what one has—not according to what one does not have. I do not mean that there should be relief for others and pressure on you, but it is a question of a fair balance between your present abundance and their need, so that their abundance may be for your need, in order that there may be a fair balance. As it is written, "The one who had much did not have too much, and the one who had little did not have too little"* (2 Cor. 8:12-15).

Enough is enough. Or, it should be.

One of the lessons we teach our children is that life is not fair. We do this in order to prepare them for the "real world."

This is true, as far as it goes. What we should be teaching them is, "Nevertheless, God wants us to help change this." This is God's Economics 101. As Christians, we are to reinvent the world.

I'm as much a victim of the American notion of self-reliance as anyone. I need the relief of Sabbath rest and the reminder of my stewardship responsibilities as much as anyone does. That's why the Sabbath is a time of rest. It's a reminder that our well-being does not depend upon our busy-ness, but upon God's faithfulness. As the psalmist put it, *It is in vain that you rise up early and go late to rest, eating the bread of anxious toil; for he gives sleep to his beloved* (Psalm 127).

But more importantly, the planet needs a Jubilee. We, inheritors of the Industrial Revolution, need a total reorienting of our economic priorities. We need to move away from overconsumption and toward enough is enough. We must learn to live simply so that others may simply live.

As Christians, it's time to quit paying lip-service to Jesus as Lord of our lives and follow him into a Jubilee world. The delivery mechanism of God's abundance is not magic, not directly from the hand of God, but from the hands of those who understand Sabbath Economics. Therefore, the well-being of the world depends upon those who understand this. As God's stewards of the earth's resources, it is our responsibility to make sure that we don't have too much so that others may have enough.

But we dither, we question, we doubt if there is anything to this Jubilee thing. So it was in Jesus' day: *"John the Baptist has sent us to you to ask, 'Are you the one who is to come, or are we to wait for another?'" [22] And Jesus answered them, "Go and tell John what you have seen and heard: the blind receive their sight, the lame walk, the lepers are cleansed, the deaf hear, the dead are raised, the poor have good news brought to them."*

Elton Trueblood offers this challenge to the church:

> Somewhere in the world there should be a society consciously and deliberately devoted to the task of seeing how love can be make real and demonstrating love in practice.... If God, as we believe, is truly revealed in the life of Christ, the most important thing [to God] is the creation of centers of loving

fellowship, which in turn infect the world. Whether the world can be redeemed in this way we do not know. But it is at least clear that there is no other way.[28]

Need we look for another? The right politician, perhaps, or the right movement, or maybe the right time? No. The time for waiting is over. Jubilee is here if only we have the heart to keep the Sabbath. If we do, the world will never be the same again. Enough is enough.

AMEN

---

28 Elton Trueblood, *The Company of the Committed* (New York: Harper & Brothers, 1961), p.113.

# TOPICAL LINE DRIVES

### *Straight to the Point in under 44 Pages*

All Topical Line Drives volumes are priced at $4.99 print and 99¢ in all ebook formats.

## Available

## Forthcoming

## Planned

(The titles of planned volumes may change before release.)

Generous Quantity Discounts Available
Dealer Inquiries Welcome
Energion Publications — P.O. Box 841
Gonzalez, FL 32560
Website: http://energionpubs.com
Phone: (850) 525-3916

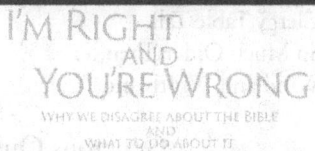

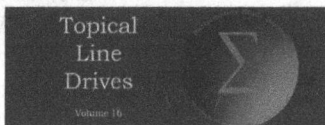

# MORE FROM ENERGION PUBLICATIONS

## Personal Study

| | | |
|---|---|---|
| Finding My Way in Christianity | Herold Weiss | $16.99 |
| The Jesus Paradigm | David Alan Black | $17.99 |
| When People Speak for God | Henry Neufeld | $17.99 |

## Christian Living

| | | |
|---|---|---|
| Faith in the Public Square | Robert D. Cornwall | $16.99 |
| Grief: Finding the Candle of Light | Jody Neufeld | $8.99 |
| Crossing the Street | Robert LaRochelle | $16.99 |

## Bible Study

| | | |
|---|---|---|
| Learning and Living Scripture | Lentz/Neufeld | $12.99 |
| From Inspiration to Understanding | Edward W. H. Vick | $24.99 |
| Luke: A Participatory Study Guide | Geoffrey Lentz | $8.99 |
| Philippians: A Participatory Study Guide | Bruce Epperly | $9.99 |
| Ephesians: A Participatory Study Guide | Robert D. Cornwall | $9.99 |
| Evidence for the Bible | Elgin Hushbeck, Jr. | $16.99 |
| When People Speak for God | Henry Neufeld | $17.99 |
| Meditations on According to John | Herold Weiss | $14.99 |

## Theology

| | | |
|---|---|---|
| Creation in Scripture | Herold Weiss | $12.99 |
| Creation: the Christian Doctrine | Edward W. H. Vick | $12.99 |
| Ultimate Allegiance | Robert D. Cornwall | $9.99 |
| History and Christian Faith | Edward W. H. Vick | $9.99 |
| The Journey to the Undiscovered Country | William Powell Tuck | $9.99 |
| Philosophy for Believers | Edward W. H. Vick | $14.99 |

## Ministry

| | | |
|---|---|---|
| Clergy Table Talk | Kent Ira Groff | $9.99 |
| So Much Older Then ... | Robert LaRochelle | $9.99 |
| Wind and Whirlwind | David Moffett-Moore | $9.99 |

Generous Quantity Discounts Available
Dealer Inquiries Welcome
Energion Publications — P.O. Box 841
Gonzalez, FL 32560
Website: http://energionpubs.com
Phone: (850) 525-3916

www.ingramcontent.com/pod-product-compliance
Lightning Source LLC
Chambersburg PA
CBHW011748020426
42331CB00014B/3323